My Beautiful Broken Shell

began in 1982, shortly after my husband,
Steve, was diagnosed with multiple sclerosis.
I felt frightened...discouraged...alone.

I went to the beach one day and decided to
gather a few shells for my collection. The
first one I picked up was a broken scallop
shell, so I threw it back. But then I picked it
up again and saw myself as I was at that
moment...broken, too...just like the shell.

God spoke to me about my brokenness, and
these reflections have helped me and many
others get through difficult times. My deepest
wish is that you always know how truly
beautiful you are...not despite your
brokenness...but beca

Carol

*My Beautiful
Broken Shell*

Copyright © 1999 by Carol Hamblet Adams

Published by Garborg's, Inc.
P. O. Box 20132, Bloomington, MN 55420

Illustrated by Craig Lueck
Design by Shelby Davis

Scripture quotations marked NIV are taken from
the HOLY BIBLE, NEW INTERNATIONAL
VERSION®. Copyright © 1973, 1978, 1984 by
International Bible Society. Used by permission of
Zondervan Publishing House.

Scripture quotations marked TLB are taken from
THE LIVING BIBLE, Copyright © 1971. Used by
permission of Tyndale House Publishers, Inc.,
Wheaton, IL 60189. All rights reserved.

Scripture quotations marked MSG are taken from
THE MESSAGE. Copyright © 1993, 1994, 1995,
1996. Used by permission of NavPress
Publishing Group.

ISBN 1-58375-534-9

The waves echo behind me.
Patience—Faith—Openness, is
what the sea has to teach.
Simplicity—Solitude.... But there
are other beaches to explore.
There are more shells to find.
This is only a beginning.

ANNE MORROW LINDBERGH

JANUARY 1

*L*ord...give me the gift of faith to be renewed and shared with others each day. Teach me to live this moment only, looking neither to the past with regret, nor the future with apprehension. Let love be my aim and my life a prayer.

ROSEANN ALEXANDER-ISHAM

DECEMBER 31

*L*ord, as I come to the "shore" today, I am grateful for the peace and calm of this moment where time stands still and I am able to share a few quiet thoughts.

CAROL HAMBLET ADAMS

JANUARY 2

My Presence will go with you,
and I will give you rest.

EXODUS 33:14 NIV

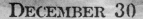

DECEMBER 30

$\mathcal{T}$here is a past which is gone
forever, but there is a future
which is still our own.

F. W. ROBERTSON

JANUARY 3

*G*od may be invisible, but He's in touch. You may not be able to see Him, but He is in control.... That includes all of life—past, present, future.

CHARLES R. SWINDOLL

DECEMBER 29

*G*od specializes in things fresh and firsthand. His plans for you this year may outshine those of the past.... He's prepared to fill your days with reasons to give Him praise.

JONI EARECKSON TADA

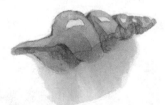

JANUARY 4

*I*f we celebrate
the years behind us
they become stepping-stones of
strength and joy for
the years ahead.

DECEMBER 28

The Lord is close to the brokenhearted and saves those who are crushed in spirit.

PSALM 34:18 NIV

JANUARY 5

God knows no distance.

CHARLESZETTA WADDLES

DECEMBER 27

*I*f peace be in the heart the
wildest winter storm is full
of solemn beauty.

C. F. RICHARDSON

JANUARY 6

How silently, how silently
The wondrous gift is given
So God imparts to
human hearts
The wonders
of His heaven.

PHILLIPS BROOKS

DECEMBER 26

*G*od comforts. He doesn't pity.
He picks us up, dries our tears,
soothes our fears, and lifts our
thoughts beyond the hurt.

DR. ROBERT SCHULLER

JANUARY 7

Behold, a virgin shall be with child, and shall bring forth a son, and they shall call his name Emmanuel...God with us.

MATTHEW 1:23 KJV

DECEMBER 25

Even in the winter, even in the midst of the storm, the sun is still there. Somewhere, up above the clouds, it still shines and warms and pulls at the life buried deep inside the brown branches and frozen earth. The sun is there! Spring will come! The clouds cannot stay forever.

GLORIA GAITHER

JANUARY 8

God must have said, "I know what I'll do, I'll send my love right down there where they are. And I'll send it as a tiny baby so they'll have to touch it and they'll have to hold it close."

GLORIA GAITHER

DECEMBER 24

Today I'll remember that
by God's grace I am
all I need to be.

*C*hristmas is a time of the
heart, not just a date. Its meaning
transcends time. Jesus was born
to love us and fill our
lives with Himself.

God...comforts us in all our troubles, so that we can comfort those in any trouble with the comfort we ourselves have received from God.

2 CORINTHIANS 1:3-4 NIV

JANUARY 10

$\mathcal{G}$od grant you the light in Christmas, which is faith; the warmth of Christmas, which is love...the belief in Christmas, which is truth; the all of Christmas, which is Christ.

WILDA ENGLISH

DECEMBER 22

*H*ope is not
the conviction
that something
will turn out well,
but the certainty that something
makes sense regardless of
how it turns out.

BARBARA JOHNSON

JANUARY 11

At this special time of year:
Follow the children. Hear the joy
in their laughter. See the love in
their eyes. Feel the hope
in their touch.

DECEMBER 21

*W*e all mold one another's dreams. We all hold each other's fragile hopes in our hands. We all touch others' hearts.

JANUARY 12

$\mathcal{G}$od is our refuge and strength,
an ever-present help in trouble.
Therefore we will not fear.... The
Lord Almighty is with us.

PSALM 46:1-2,7 NIV

DECEMBER 20

My life is but a weaving
between my Lord and me,
I cannot choose the colors
He worketh steadily...
The dark threads are as needful
in the Weaver's skillful hand
As the threads of gold and silver
in the pattern He has planned.

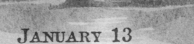

JANUARY 13

*Christmas is the celebration of
the keeping of a promise....
A saving promise.*

MICHAEL CARD

DECEMBER 19

*G*od has a wonderful plan for each person He has chosen. He knew even before He created this world what beauty He would bring forth from our lives.

LOUIS B. WYLY

JANUARY 14

Christmas is...
A gift from heaven above.
Christmas is hope.
Christmas is love.

DECEMBER 18

*B*e beautiful inside, in your hearts, with the lasting charm of a gentle and quiet spirit which is so precious to God.

1 PETER 3:4 TLB

JANUARY 15

As I look once more at the broken scallop shell in my hand, I am reminded of all the beautiful shells God has placed around me.

Lord, may I truly value every moment spent with my loved ones.

CAROL HAMBLET ADAMS

DECEMBER 17

As I walk along the beach picking up shells, I see that each one has its own special beauty...its own unique pattern.

Thank You, Lord, for embracing my shell...whether I am whole or broken.

CAROL HAMBLET ADAMS

JANUARY 16

The guardian angels of life sometimes fly so high as to be beyond our sight, but they are always looking down upon us.

JEAN PAUL RICHTER

DECEMBER 16

Even if our tears are for ourselves, for our ache of loneliness, for our pain of loss, they are...sacred, for they are tears of our love.

RABBI JACK STERN JR.

JANUARY 17

*G*od can do anything, you
know—far more than you could
ever imagine or guess or request
in your wildest dreams!

EPHESIANS 3:20 MSG

DECEMBER 15

*G*od loves and cares for us,
even to the least event and
smallest need of life.

HENRY EDWARD MANNING

JANUARY 18

*S*ome gifts are big, others are small. Gifts from the heart are the best gifts of all.

DECEMBER 14

*F*aith in small things has repercussions that ripple all the way out. In a huge dark room a little match can light up the place.

JONI EARECKSON TADA

JANUARY 19

*Down the dark future,
through long generations,
The echoing sounds grow
fainter and then cease;
And like a bell, with
solemn, sweet vibrations,
I hear once more the
voice of Christ say
"Peace!"*

LONGFELLOW

DECEMBER 13

*C*ast your cares on the Lord
and he will sustain you.

PSALM 55:22 NIV

JANUARY 20

$\mathcal{O}$ur Heavenly Father never takes anything from His children unless He means to give them something better.

GEORGE MUELLER

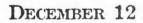

DECEMBER 12

There is only one way for you to live without grief in your lifetime; that is to exist without love. Your grief represents your humanness, just as your love does.

CAROL STANDACHER

JANUARY 21

*G*od meets our needs in
unexpected ways.

JANETTE OKE

DECEMBER 11

I am not afraid of storms for
I am learning how to sail my ship.

LOUISA MAY ALCOTT

JANUARY 22

*M*ay the God of hope
fill you with all joy
and peace as you
trust in him.

ROMANS 15:13 NIV

DECEMBER 10

*W*here the soul is full of peace
and joy, outward surroundings
and circumstances are of
comparatively little account.

HANNAH WHITALL SMITH

JANUARY 23

*W*inter preserves and strengthens a tree. Rather than expending its strength on the exterior surface, the tree forces its sap deeper into its interior. In winter a tougher, more resilient life is firmly established. Winter is necessary for the tree to survive and flourish.

RICHARD J. FOSTER

DECEMBER 9

*M*ay you wake
each day with God's
blessings and sleep each
night in His keeping,
and may you always walk
in His tender care.

JANUARY 24

Day-to-day living becomes a window through which we get a glimpse of life eternal. The eternal illuminates and gives focus to the daily.

JANICE RIGGLE HUIE

DECEMBER 8

*D*on't you know [God] enjoys
giving rest to those
he loves?

PSALM 127:2 MSG

JANUARY 25

*S*ometimes we look so intently
toward the top of our mountain
that we stumble over the steps
leading to it. The journey begins
just where you are with
blessings in every step.

DECEMBER 7

*I*f we had no winter, the spring would not be so pleasant: if we did not sometimes taste of adversity, prosperity would not be so welcome.

ANNE BRADSTREET

JANUARY 26

*The stars are constantly shining,
but often we do not see them
until the dark hours.*

EARL RINEY

DECEMBER 6

Contentment is
not the fulfillment of
what you want, but the realization
of how much you already have.

JANUARY 27

*T*he Lord is...full of kindness. He
is close to all who call on him
sincerely.... He hears their cries for
help and rescues them. He protects
all those who love him.

PSALM 145:17-20 TLB

DECEMBER 5

*M*ay happiness touch your life
today as warmly as you
have touched the
lives of others.

JANUARY 28

As we grow in our capacities to see and enjoy the joys that God has placed in our lives, life becomes a glorious experience of discovering His endless wonders.

DECEMBER 4

$\mathcal{B}$e on the lookout for mercies.
The more we look for them,
the more of them we will
see. Blessings brighten
when we count them.

MALTBIE D. BABCOCK

JANUARY 29

*T*he most precious gifts are
wrapped in love.

DECEMBER 3

$\mathcal{G}$od takes care of all who
stay close to him.

Psalm 31:23 msg

JANUARY 30

All the darkness in the world
cannot extinguish the light
of a single candle.

MARIA GAUTIER

DECEMBER 2

*Y*ou can come out of the furnace of trouble two ways: if you let it consume you, you come out a cinder; but there is a kind of metal which refuses to be consumed, and comes out a star.

JEAN CHURCH

JANUARY 31

*Thank You for holding me
in the palm of Your hand...for
keeping me safe from
the pounding surf.*

CAROL HAMBLET ADAMS

DECEMBER 1

I stop and pick up a broken scallop shell and realize that this shell is me when my heart is broken, when I am hurting. Yet this shell is still out on the beautiful sandy shore...just as I am. *Thank you, Lord, that I haven't been completely crushed by the heaviness in my heart.*

CAROL HAMBLET ADAMS

FEBRUARY 1

$\mathcal{D}$o not fear, for I am with you;
do not be dismayed, for I am your
God. I will strengthen you and
help you; I will uphold you with
my righteous right hand.

ISAIAH 41:10 NIV

NOVEMBER 30

May you have warm words on
a cold evening, a full moon on a
dark night, and the road downhill
all the way to your door.

IRISH BLESSING

FEBRUARY 2

*I*f I cannot do great things, I can do small things in a great way.

NOVEMBER 29

Lord, help me to see my own beautiful pattern...and to remember that each line and each color on my shell was put there by You. Help me to not compare myself to others, so that I may appreciate my own uniqueness.

CAROL HAMBLET ADAMS

FEBRUARY 3

No light that was born in love
can ever be extinguished.

DR. DARCIE D. SIMS

NOVEMBER 28

Love knows no limit to its endurance, no end to its trust, no fading of its hope; it can outlast anything. Love never fails.

1 CORINTHIANS 13:7-8 PHILLIPS

FEBRUARY 4

Each day of life is a precious gift from God.

CHARLES H. SPURGEON

NOVEMBER 27

Just as there comes a warm
sunbeam into every cottage
window, so comes a love—born of
God's care for every separate need.

NATHANIEL HAWTHORNE

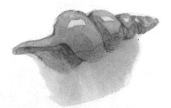

FEBRUARY 5

I have
learned from
experience that
the greater part of
our happiness or misery depends
on our dispositions and not
on our circumstances.

MARTHA WASHINGTON

NOVEMBER 26

*A*ll God's glory and beauty come from within, and there He delights to dwell. His visits there are frequent, His conversation sweet, His comforts refreshing, His peace passing all understanding.

THOMAS À KEMPIS

FEBRUARY 6

*O*h, give thanks to the Lord, for
He is good; His love and His
kindness go on forever.

1 CHRONICLES 16:34 TLB

NOVEMBER 25

*Y*ou are...infinitely dear to the
Father, unspeakably precious
to Him. You are never, not
for one second, alone.

NORMAN F. DOWTY

FEBRUARY 7

I would maintain that thanks are the highest form of thought, and that gratitude is happiness doubled by wonder.

G. K. CHESTERTON

NOVEMBER 24

God takes life's pieces and gives us unbroken peace.

GOUGH

FEBRUARY 8

*A*s we grow in our capacities to see and enjoy the joys that God has placed in our lives, life becomes a glorious experience of discovering His endless wonders.

NOVEMBER 23

*G*od guards you from every evil, he guards your very life. He guards you when you leave and when you return, he guards you now, he guards you always.

PSALM 121:7-8 MSG

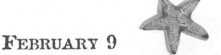

FEBRUARY 9

*G*od is not too great to
be concerned about our
smallest wishes.

BASILEA SCHLINK

NOVEMBER 22

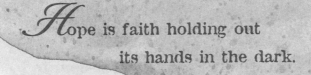

*H*ope is faith holding out
its hands in the dark.

GEORGE ILES

FEBRUARY 10

*I*n those times I can't seem to find God, I rest in the assurance He knows how to find me.

NEVA COYLE

NOVEMBER 21

There are times when
encouragement means such
a lot. And a word is enough
to convey it.

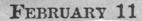

FEBRUARY 11

May your roots go down deep
into the soil of God's marvelous
love; and may you be able to feel
and understand...how long, how
wide, how deep, and how high his
love really is; and to experience
this love for yourselves, though it
is so great that you will never
see the end of it.

EPHESIANS 3:17-19 TLB

NOVEMBER 20

*C*herish your visions; cherish your ideals; cherish the music that stirs in your heart, the beauty that forms in your mind, the loveliness that drapes your purest thoughts, for out of them will grow all delightful conditions, all heavenly environment.

JAMES ALLEN

FEBRUARY 12

Don't be afraid. God is for you.

BILLY GRAHAM

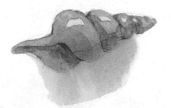

NOVEMBER 19

*W*hen you are in the dark,
listen, and God will give you a
very precious message for
someone else when you
get into the light.

OSWALD CHAMBERS

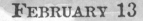

FEBRUARY 13

$\mathcal{G}$rief knits two hearts in closer bonds than happiness ever can; and common sufferings are far stronger links than common joys.

ALPHONSE DE LAMARTINE

NOVEMBER 18

*D*on't be afraid, for I...have
called you by name; you are mine.
When you go through deep waters
and great trouble, I will
be with you.

ISAIAH 43:1-2 TLB

FEBRUARY 14

*G*od's hand is always there;
once you grasp it, you'll never
want to let it go.

NOVEMBER 17

*A*ll the beautiful sentiments
in the world weigh less than
a simple lovely action.

JAMES RUSSELL LOWELL

FEBRUARY 15

The Lord will guide you always; he will satisfy your needs.... You will be like a well-watered garden, like a spring whose waters never fail.

ISAIAH 58:11 NIV

NOVEMBER 16

The God who created the vast
resources of the universe is also
the inventor of the human mind.
His inspired words of
encouragement guarantee us
that we can live above
our circumstances.

DR. JAMES DOBSON

FEBRUARY 16

*L*et me not destroy the beauty
of today by grieving over
yesterday...or worrying about
tomorrow. May I cherish and
appreciate my shell collection
each and every day.

CAROL HAMBLET ADAMS

NOVEMBER 15

Thank You, Lord, for hope in times of despair...for light in times of darkness...for patience in times of suffering. For assuring me that with You all things are possible.

CAROL HAMBLET ADAMS

FEBRUARY 17

*H*ope means to keep living
amid desperation and to keep
humming in the darkness.

HENRI J. M. NOUWEN

NOVEMBER 14

*P*rayer is the key of the
morning and the bolt on
the door at night.

FEBRUARY 18

$\mathcal{A}$ thankful person can find
contentment anywhere.

NOVEMBER 13

The Lord is faithful to all his
promises and loving toward
all he has made.

PSALM 145:13 NIV

FEBRUARY 19

*C*ontentment comes as the infallible result of great acceptances, great humilities—of not trying to make ourselves this or that, but of surrendering ourselves to the fullness of life—of letting life flow through us.

DAVID GRAYSON

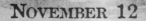

NOVEMBER 12

*Y*ou pay God a compliment by asking great things of Him.

TERESA OF AVILA

FEBRUARY 20

He loves each one of us, as if there were only one of us.

AUGUSTINE

NOVEMBER 11

*W*hen we do the best that we can, we never know what miracle is wrought in our life, or in the life of another.

HELEN KELLER

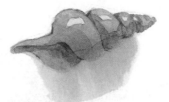

FEBRUARY 21

$\mathcal{F}$or I know
the plans I have
for you," declares
the Lord, "plans to
prosper you and not to harm you,
plans to give you hope
and a future."

JEREMIAH 29:11 NIV

NOVEMBER 10

*C*omfort and prosperity have never enriched the world as adversity has done. Out of pain and problems have come the sweetest songs, the most poignant poems, the most gripping stories. Out of suffering and tears have come the greatest spirits and the most blessed lives.

BILLY GRAHAM

FEBRUARY 22

*G*od makes a promise—faith believes it, hope anticipates it, patience quietly awaits it.

NOVEMBER 9

$\mathcal{F}$aith is the centerpiece of a
connected life. It allows us to live
by the grace of invisible strands. It
is a belief in a wisdom superior to
our own. Faith becomes a teacher
in the absence of fact.

TERRY TEMPEST WILLIAMS

FEBRUARY 23

I have held many things in my hands and I have lost them all; but whatever I have placed in God's hands, that I still possess.

MARTIN LUTHER

NOVEMBER 8

*D*on't be anxious about tomorrow. God will take care of your tomorrow too. Live one day at a time.

MATTHEW 6:34 TLB

FEBRUARY 24

$\mathcal{G}$od will lift up
all who have a humble
spirit and save them in all
trials and tribulations.

THOMAS À KEMPIS

NOVEMBER 7

*H*ope sees the
invisible, feels the
intangible, and achieves
the impossible.

FEBRUARY 25

*T*he true way of softening one's
troubles is to solace
those of others.

MADAME DE MAINTENON

NOVEMBER 6

God gives me new life—not just for today, but for tomorrow and every day after that.

FEBRUARY 26

*F*or your lovingkindness is great
beyond measure, high as the
heavens. Your faithfulness
reaches the skies.

PSALM 108:4 TLB

NOVEMBER 5

There is no safer place to be
than in God's loving hands.

FEBRUARY 27

The most extraordinary thing about the oyster is this. Irritations get into the shell.... And when he cannot get rid of them, he uses the irritations to do the loveliest thing an oyster ever has the chance to do. If there are irritations in our lives today, there is only one prescription: make a pearl.... And it takes faith and love to do it.

HARRY EMERSON FOSDICK

NOVEMBER 4

*E*ven when all
we see are the
tangled threads on the backside
of life's tapestry, we know that
God is good and is out to
do us good always.

RICHARD J. FOSTER

FEBRUARY 28

*I*t's the little things that make
up the richest part of the
tapestry of our lives.

NOVEMBER 3

O Lord, be gracious to us; we long for you. Be our strength every morning, our salvation in time of distress.

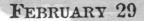

ISAIAH 33:2 NIV

FEBRUARY 29

$\mathscr{N}$ever be afraid to trust
an unknown future to an
all-knowing God.

CORRIE TEN BOOM

NOVEMBER 2

*G*od knows the rhythm of my
spirit and knows my heart
thoughts. He is as close
as breathing.

MARCH 1

*G*od's promises are like the stars; the darker the night, the brighter they shine.

DAVID NICHOLAS

NOVEMBER 1

*G*od has promised
strength for the day,
rest for the labor,
light for the way,
grace for the trials,
help from above,
unfailing sympathy,
undying love.

ANNIE JOHNSON FLINT

MARCH 2

He heals the heartbroken.... He counts the stars and assigns each a name. Our Lord is great, with limitless strength; we'll never comprehend what he knows and does.

PSALM 147:3-5 MSG

OCTOBER 31

*G*od will never let you be
shaken or moved from your
place near His heart.

JONI EARECKSON TADA

MARCH 3

May I always take the time to watch a kite dance in the sky...to sing...to pick daisies...to love...to take risks...to believe in my dreams.

CAROL HAMBLET ADAMS

OCTOBER 30

$\mathcal{I}$f our world were only filled
with perfect shells, we would miss
some of life's most important
lessons along the way.

CAROL HAMBLET ADAMS

MARCH 4

In waiting we begin to get in touch with the rhythms of life—stillness and action, listening and decision. They are the rhythms of God. It is in the everyday and the commonplace that we learn patience, acceptance, and contentment.

RICHARD J. FOSTER

OCTOBER 29

*I*t is love that asks, that seeks, that knocks, that finds, and that is faithful to what it finds.

AUGUSTINE

MARCH 5

When we wrap our arms
around those who sorrow, we do
so on behalf of Jesus, who would
do it if He were here.

JANETTE OKE

OCTOBER 28

$\mathcal{B}$lessed are those who mourn,
for they will be comforted.

MATTHEW 5:4 NIV

MARCH 6

God can do wonders with
a broken heart if you give
Him all the pieces.

VICTOR ALFSEN

OCTOBER 27

I have seen what a laugh can do. It can transform almost unbearable tears into something bearable, even hopeful.

BOB HOPE

MARCH 7

The steadfast love of the Lord never ceases, his mercies never come to an end; they are new every morning; great is your faithfulness.

LAMENTATIONS 3:22-23 NRSV

OCTOBER 26

*I*f you have a special need today, focus your full attention on the goodness and greatness of God rather than on the size of your need. Your need is so small compared to God's ability to meet it.

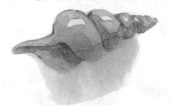

MARCH 8

*I*f Winter comes, can Spring be far behind?

PERCY BYSSHE SHELLEY

OCTOBER 25

When you get to the end of
your rope, tie a knot and hang
on—and then swing.

BARBARA JOHNSON

MARCH 9

*W*e come closest to God at
our lowest moments.

TERRY ANDERSON

OCTOBER 24

I have loved you with an everlasting love; I have drawn you with loving-kindness.

JEREMIAH 31:3 NIV

MARCH 10

The soul would have no rainbow
had the eye no tear.

OCTOBER 23

*G*od is, and all is well.

JOHN GREENLEAF WHITTIER

MARCH 11

*N*ight by night I
will lie down and sleep in
the thought of God.

WILLIAM MOUNTFORD

OCTOBER 22

*F*or yesterday is
but a dream and
tomorrow is only a vision.
But today well lived makes
every yesterday a dream of
happiness and tomorrow
a vision of hope.

KÁLIDÁSA

MARCH 12

*I*nstead of worrying, pray. Let petitions and praises shape your worries into prayers, letting God know your concerns. Before you know it, a sense of God's wholeness, everything coming together for good, will come and settle you down.

PHILIPPIANS 4:6-7 MSG

OCTOBER 21

*R*egardless of the need, God comforts. He is the God of all comfort! That's His specialty.

CHARLES R. SWINDOLL

MARCH 13

*G*od's forgiveness and love
exist for you as if you were
the only person on earth.

CECIL OSBORNE

OCTOBER 20

Time is a dressmaker
specializing in alterations.

FAITH BALDWIN

MARCH 14

*T*ry to see the beauty "in your own backyard," to notice the miracles of everyday life.

GLORIA GAITHER

OCTOBER 19

$\mathcal{Y}$ou are my
hiding place; you
will protect me from
trouble and surround me with
songs of deliverance.

PSALM 32:7 NIV

MARCH 15

$\mathscr{W}$e must accept finite disappointment, but we must never lose infinite hope.

BARBARA JOHNSON

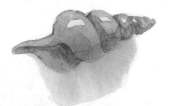

OCTOBER 18

*G*od loves us for ourselves. He
values our love more than
He values galaxies of
new created worlds.

A. W. TOZER

MARCH 16

*E*ach dawn holds a new hope
for a new plan, making the start
of each day the start of a new life.

GINA BLAIR

OCTOBER 17

We may ask, "why does God bring thunderclouds and disasters when we want green pastures and still waters?" Bit by bit, we find behind the clouds, the Father's feet; behind the thunder, a still small voice that comforts with a comfort that is unspeakable.

OSWALD CHAMBERS

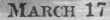

MARCH 17

You're my cave to hide in, my cliff to climb. Be my safe leader, be my true mountain guide. Free me from hidden traps; I want to hide in you. I've put my life in your hands. You won't drop me, you'll never let me down.

PSALM 31:3-5 MSG

OCTOBER 16

*W*hat the heart has
once owned and had,
it shall never lose.

HENRY WARD BEECHER

MARCH 18

*W*e can put our minds at ease
because God's mind is on us.

OCTOBER 15

Come to me, all you who are weary and burdened, and I will give you rest. Take my yoke upon you and learn from me, for I am gentle and humble in heart, and you will find rest for your souls. For my yoke is easy and my burden is light.

MATTHEW 11:28-30 NIV

MARCH 19

May I always wonder at the shell in the sand...the dawn of a new day...the beauty of a flower...the blessing of a friend...the love of a child.

CAROL HAMBLET ADAMS

OCTOBER 14

Thank you, Lord, for all that I learn from my brokenness...for the courage it takes to live with my pain...and for the strength it takes to remain on the shore.

CAROL HAMBLET ADAMS

MARCH 20

*W*hatever the circumstances, whatever the call, whatever the duty, whatever the price, whatever the sacrifice—His strength will be your strength in your hour of need.

BILLY GRAHAM

OCTOBER 13

*L*ife is what we are alive to. It is not length but breadth.... Be alive to...goodness, kindness, purity, love, history, poetry, music, flowers, stars, God, and eternal hope.

MALTBIE D. BABCOCK

MARCH 21

*G*od's peace is joy resting. His joy is peace dancing.

F. F. BRUCE

OCTOBER 12

*W*hen faith is strong, troubles become trifles. There can be comfort in sorrow because in the midst of mourning, God gives a song.

BILLY GRAHAM

MARCH 22

I am still confident of this: I will see the goodness of the Lord in the land of the living. Wait for the Lord; be strong and take heart and wait for the Lord.

PSALM 27:13-14 NIV

OCTOBER 11

*T*hose who don't know how to weep with their whole heart don't know how to laugh either.

GOLDA MEIR

MARCH 23

The value of a person is not measured on an applause meter; it is measured in the heart and mind of God.

JOHN FISCHER

OCTOBER 10

*L*ook for the heaven here on earth. It is all around you.

MARCH 24

The world is
full of suffering. It
is also full of the overcoming of it.

HELEN KELLER

OCTOBER 9

*H*ow precious it is, Lord, to realize that you are thinking about me constantly! I can't even count how many times a day your thoughts turn towards me.

PSALM 139:17 TLB

MARCH 25

I see skies of blue, and
clouds of white
Bright blessed days, and
dark sacred nights
and I think to myself,
"What a wonderful world."

WEISS AND THEILE

OCTOBER 8

*H*aving someone who understands is a great blessing for ourselves. Being someone who understands is a great blessing to others.

JANETTE OKE

MARCH 26

Though our feelings come and go, God's love for us does not.

C. S. LEWIS

OCTOBER 7

*I*n time we can accept a great
loss if we have somebody loving
us through it. God sends friends
and companions to love
and support us.

DR. ROBERT SCHULLER

MARCH 27

*T*he eternal God
is your refuge, and
underneath are the
everlasting arms.

DEUTERONOMY 33:27 NIV

OCTOBER 6

*H*ave courage
for the great sorrows of
life, and patience for the
small ones; and when you
have...accomplished your daily
task, go to sleep in peace.
God is awake.

VICTOR HUGO

MARCH 28

*L*ife without emotion [is] like
an engine without fuel.

MARY ASTOR

OCTOBER 5

*T*aken separately,
the experiences of life can work
harm and not good. Taken
together, they make a
pattern of blessing
and strength
the like of
which the world
does not know.

V. RAYMOND EDMAN

MARCH 29

I have been trying to make
the best of grief and am just
beginning to learn to allow it
to make the best of me.

BARBARA LAZEAR ASCHER

OCTOBER 4

*Y*our heavenly Father knows
your needs. He will always give
you all you need from day to day.

LUKE 12:30-31 TLB

MARCH 30

*G*od is every moment totally aware of each one of us. Totally aware in intense concentration and love.... No one passes through any area of life, happy or tragic, without the attention of God.

EUGENIA PRICE

OCTOBER 3

*T*rue worth is

in *being*, not *seeming*—

In doing, each day that goes by,

Some little good—not in dreaming

Of great things to do by and by.

ALICE CARY

MARCH 31

$\mathscr{A}$ caring heart and a simple
deed can relieve another's grief.

JANETTE OKE

OCTOBER 2

The year's at the spring
And day's at the morn...
God's in His heaven—
All's right with
the world!

ROBERT BROWNING

APRIL 1

*T*hough I walk through the valley of the shadow of death, I will fear no evil: for thou art with me; thy rod and thy staff they comfort me.

PSALM 23:4 KJV

OCTOBER 1

*A*s Jesus stepped into the garden, you were in His prayers. As Jesus looked into heaven, you were in His vision.... His final prayer was about you. His final pain was for you. His final passion was you.

MAX LUCADO

APRIL 2

*A*mong God's best gifts to us
are the people who love us.

SEPTEMBER 30

*M*ay the Lord bless and
protect you; may the Lord's face
radiate with joy because of you;
may he be gracious to you,
show you his favor, and
give you his peace.

NUMBERS 6:24-26 TLB

APRIL 3

*D*on't be ashamed to be a child
in your relationship to God. Let
the everlasting arms rock you to
sleep.... He will take care of you
day and night, forever.

NORMAN VINCENT PEALE

SEPTEMBER 29

*T*he only courage that matters
is the kind that gets you from
one moment to the next.

MIGNON MCLAUGHLIN

APRIL 4

Lord, help me to remain childlike in my appreciation for life. Please slow me down... that I may always see the extraordinary in the ordinary.

CAROL HAMBLET ADAMS

SEPTEMBER 28

*B*roken shells teach us not to look at our imperfections...but to look at the beauty...the great beauty...of what is still left.

Help me to truly accept myself just as I am, Lord, so that I may sing the song in my heart...for no one else has my song to sing... my gift to give.

CAROL HAMBLET ADAMS

APRIL 5

$\mathcal{I}$f you can help anybody even
a little, be glad; up the steps of
usefulness and kindness, God will
lead you on to happiness
and friendship.

MALTBIE D. BABCOCK

SEPTEMBER 27

*F*aith believes that God
will plant the seeds of hope for
tomorrow in the garden
of our hearts today.

JANET L. WEAVER

APRIL 6

The Lord gives strength to his people; the Lord blesses his people with peace.

PSALM 29:11 NIV

SEPTEMBER 26

God sends the brilliant light of
a rainbow to remind us
of His presence.

VERDELL DAVIS

APRIL 7

*L*et my soul take
refuge...beneath the shadow of
Your wings: let my heart, this sea
of restless waves, find peace
in You, O God.

AUGUSTINE

SEPTEMBER 25

*W*e have been in God's thought
from all eternity, and in His
creative love, His attention
never leaves us.

MICHAEL QUOIST

APRIL 8

*E*ach moment contains
a hundred messages from God.
To each cry of "Oh Lord," God
answers, "I am here."

RUMI

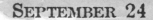

SEPTEMBER 24

I call on you, O God, for you will answer me.... Keep me as the apple of your eye; hide me in the shadow of your wings.

Psalm 17:6,8 NIV

April 9

$\mathcal{T}$he uncertainties
of the present always give way to
the enchanted possibilities
of the future.

KIRKLAND

SEPTEMBER 23

The joyful birds
prolong the strain,
their song with every
spring renewed;
the air we breathe,
and falling rain,
each softly whispers:
God is good.

JOHN HAMPDEN GURNEY

APRIL 10

*N*othing great was ever done
without much enduring.

CATHERINE OF SIENNA

SEPTEMBER 22

*K*eep your face to the sunshine
and you cannot see the shadows.

HELEN KELLER

APRIL 11

*C*all upon me in the day of
trouble; I will deliver
you, and you
will honor me.

PSALM 50:15 NIV

SEPTEMBER 21

*E*ach one of us is God's
special work of art.

JONI EARECKSON TADA

APRIL 12

*G*od's care for
us is more watchful
and more tender than
the care of any human
father could possibly be.

HANNAH WHITALL SMITH

SEPTEMBER 20

*W*hat lies behind
us and what lies before us
are tiny matters, compared
to what lies within us.

RALPH WALDO EMERSON

APRIL 13

*E*arth has no sorrow that
Heaven cannot heal.

THOMAS MOORE

SEPTEMBER 19

What a wonderful God we
have—he is...the source of
every mercy, and
the one who
so wonderfully
comforts and
strengthens us.

2 Corinthians 1:3 tlb

April 14

*T*hose we hold most dear never
leave us. They live on in the
kindness they showed, the comfort
they shared, and the love
they brought into...life.

Norton

September 18

*D*on't fear tomorrow,

God is already there.

APRIL 15

The stronger the winds, the deeper the roots, and the longer the winds, the more beautiful the tree.

CHARLES R. SWINDOLL

SEPTEMBER 17

If you can
learn to laugh
in spite of the
circumstances that surround you,
you will enrich others, enrich
yourself, and more than
that, you will last.

BARBARA JOHNSON

APRIL 16

I love the Lord because he hears my prayers and answers them. Because he bends down and listens, I will pray as long as I breathe!

PSALM 116:1-2 TLB

SEPTEMBER 16

There is no unbelief;
Whoever plants
a seed beneath the sod
And waits to see it push
away the clod,
He trusts in God.

ELIZABETH YORK CASE

APRIL 17

$\mathcal{G}$od's heart is the most sensitive and tender of all. No act goes unnoticed, no matter how insignificant or small.

RICHARD J. FOSTER

SEPTEMBER 15

*L*ove requires sharing,
sharing requires struggle,
struggle requires faith,
faith requires love.

APRIL 18

$\mathcal{F}$ind a place or an activity that gives your senses a chance to unwind and lets you catch a fresh vision of peacetime possibilities. Furnish it comfortably. Make it beautiful. Use it often.

THOMAS KINKADE

SEPTEMBER 14

*Y*our thoughts—how rare, how beautiful! God, I'll never comprehend them! I couldn't even begin to count them—any more than I could count the sand of the sea.

PSALM 139:17-18 MSG

APRIL 19

God possesses infinite knowledge and an awareness which is uniquely His. At all times, even in the midst of any type of suffering, I can realize that He knows, loves, watches, understands, and more than that, He has a purpose.

BILLY GRAHAM

SEPTEMBER 13

*S*nuggle in God's arms. When you are hurting, when you feel lonely...let Him cradle you, comfort you, reassure you of His all-sufficient power and love.

KAY ARTHUR

APRIL 20

*S*omehow...I receive so many gifts. I am grateful for the inner peace that fills my soul.

CAROL HAMBLET ADAMS

SEPTEMBER 12

Broken shells represent tears, pain, struggle...but they are also valuable for teaching faith, courage, and strength.

Thank You for the precious gift of faith that keeps me strong when I am weak...that keeps me going when it would be easier to quit.

CAROL HAMBLET ADAMS

APRIL 21

*H*e is like a father to us,
tender and sympathetic.... The
lovingkindness of the Lord is
from everlasting to everlasting,
to those who reverence him.

PSALM 103:13,17 TLB

SEPTEMBER 11

*T*he wonder of living is held within the beauty of silence, the glory of sunlight...the sweetness of fresh spring air, the quiet strength of earth, and the love that lies at the very root of all things.

APRIL 22

*I*t is only with the heart that one can see rightly. What is essential is invisible to the eye.

ANTOINE DE SAINT-EXUPÉRY

SEPTEMBER 10

$\mathcal{T}$o gain that which is worth
having, it may be necessary
to lose everything else.

BERNADETTE DEVLIN

APRIL 23

*T*here is no limit to God's love.
It is without measure and its
depth cannot be sounded.

MOTHER TERESA

SEPTEMBER 9

*S*ince God assured us, "I'll never let you down, never walk off and leave you," we can boldly quote, "God is there, ready to help."

HEBREWS 13:5-6 MSG

APRIL 24

*S*orrows come to stretch
out spaces in the
heart for joy.

EDWIN MARKHAM

SEPTEMBER 8

*G*od wants us to lay our
burdens on Him and rest in
His love. It's His responsibility
to work out the purpose and
plan in our hardships.

JONI EARECKSON TADA

APRIL 25

*D*o you
believe that God
is near? He wants
you to. He wants
you to know that He is in the
midst of your world. Wherever you
are as you read these words, He
is present.... And He is more
than near. He is active.

MAX LUCADO

SEPTEMBER 7

May you be ever present in
the garden of God's love.

APRIL 26

I will lie down and sleep in peace, for you alone, O Lord, make me dwell in safety.

PSALM 4:8 NIV

SEPTEMBER 6

There is a sacredness in tears.
They are not the mark of
weakness, but of power. They
speak more eloquently than
10,000 tongues. They are the
messengers of overwhelming
grief, of deep contrition, and
of unspeakable love.

Washington Irving

April 27

That we are alive today is proof positive that God has something for us to do today.

ANNA R. B. LINDSAY

SEPTEMBER 5

Because of you, I love a little more. Because of you, I take time to give an extra kiss good-bye. Because of you, I have a new favorite song.... Because of you, I live today, before I worry about tomorrow.... Because of you, now I can help or listen more. Because of you, today, I am me.

Eileen Wernsman

APRIL 28

*T*ime is a very
precious gift of God;
so precious that it's only
given to us moment
by moment.

AMELIA BARR

SEPTEMBER 4

May you be
given more and more
of God's kindness,
peace, and love.

JUDE 1:2 TLB

APRIL 29

If you have time to open the back door in the morning while you're drinking your coffee and look at the sky or hear the chorus the birds offer, you have time for the marvelous.... Most of life is fascinating if looked at closely enough.

DIANE ACKERMAN

SEPTEMBER 3

*N*ot a sigh is breathed, not
a pain felt, not a grief
pierces the soul, but
the throb
vibrates to
the Father's heart.

ELLEN G. WHITE

APRIL 30

There's not a place on
earth's vast round,
In ocean's deep or air
Where love and beauty
are not found,
For God is everywhere.

SEPTEMBER 2

*H*e paints the lilies of the field,
perfumes each lily bell;
If He so loves the little flowers,
I know He loves me well.

MAY 1

I will trust and not be afraid,
for the Lord is my strength
and song.

Isaiah 12:2 TLB

September 1

*A*fter winter comes the summer. After night comes the dawn. And after every storm, there comes clear, open skies.

SAMUEL RUTHERFORD

MAY 2

*G*od understands our prayers
even when we can't find
the words to say them.

AUGUST 31

The splendor of the rose and the whiteness of the lily do not rob the little violet of its scent nor the daisy of its simple charm. If every tiny flower wanted to be a rose, spring would lose its loveliness.

THÉRÈSE OF LISIEUX

MAY 3

A teardrop on earth summons
the King of heaven.

CHARLES R. SWINDOLL

AUGUST 30

I will comfort you...as
a little one is comforted
by its mother.

ISAIAH 66:13 TLB

MAY 4

I spot a broken conch shell...white and ordinary on the outside...yet brilliant coral inside. *Lord, help me see inside the hearts of the people who touch my life...and to see their true colors.*

CAROL HAMBLET ADAMS

AUGUST 29

*H*ope is the anchor of the soul, the stimulus to action, and the incentive to achievement.

MAY 5

But you, O God, are both
tender and kind, not easily
angered, immense in love,
and you never, never quit.

PSALM 86:15 MSG

AUGUST 28

A bird does not sing because
he has an answer—he sings
because he has a song.

BARBARA JOHNSON

MAY 6

Help me remember that in my brokenness I am still whole and complete in Your sight.

CAROL HAMBLET ADAMS

AUGUST 27

*B*roken shells inspire others
and demonstrate the will to go on
in a way that no perfect shell
could ever do.

*In my brokenness, may I never
take life so seriously that I forget
to laugh along the way.*

CAROL HAMBLET ADAMS

MAY 7

I still find each day too short for all the thoughts I want to think, all the walks I want to take, all the books I want to read, and all the friends I want to see. The longer I live, the more my mind dwells upon the beauty and the wonder of the world.

JOHN BURROUGHS

AUGUST 26

How beautiful a day can be
when kindness touches it.

MAY 8

You can trust God right now to supply all your needs for today. And if your needs are more tomorrow, His supply will be greater also.

AUGUST 25

*I*t was God...who made the
garden grow in your hearts.

1 CORINTHIANS 3:6 TLB

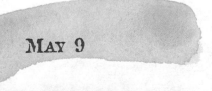

MAY 9

*M*ay God give you eyes to see
beauty only the heart
can understand.

AUGUST 24

$\mathcal{Y}$ou can't give a hug without
getting one in return.

MAY 10

I all were rain and never sun,
No bow could span the hill;
If all were sun and never rain,
There'd be no
rainbow still.

CHRISTINA ROSSETTI

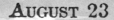

AUGUST 23

I wish you love, and strength, and faith, and wisdom, goods, gold enough to help some needy one. I wish you songs, but also blessed silence, and God's sweet peace when every day is done.

DOROTHY NELL McDONALD

MAY 11

*H*e will
wipe away all
tears from their
eyes, and there shall be no more
death, nor sorrow, nor crying, nor
pain. All of that has gone forever.

REVELATION 21:4 TLB

AUGUST 22

*Flowers never emit so sweet
and strong a fragrance as before
a storm. Beauteous soul!
when a storm approaches
thee, be as fragrant as a
sweet-smelling flower.*

JEAN PAUL RICHTER

MAY 12

*G*od goes to those who
come to Him.

RUSSIAN PROVERB

AUGUST 21

I would sooner live in a cottage
and wonder at everything than live
in a castle and wonder at nothing.

JOAN WINMILL BROWN

MAY 13

*E*very day holds the possibility
of a miracle.

AUGUST 20

I keep right on praying to you, Lord. For now is the time—you are bending down to hear! You are ready with a plentiful supply of love and kindness.

PSALM 69:13 TLB

MAY 14

If suffering went
out of life, courage,
tenderness, pity, faith,
patience, and love in its
divinity would go out of life, too.

FATHER ANDREW SDC

AUGUST 19

*D*eep down, real comfort is more important to me than temporary comfort.

JONI EARECKSON TADA

MAY 15

*L*ift up your eyes. The heavenly
Father waits to bless you—in
inconceivable ways to make
your life what you never
dreamed it could be.

ANNE ORTLUND

AUGUST 18

*T*he sun does not shine for a few trees and flowers, but for the wide world's joy.

HENRY WARD BEECHER

MAY 16

*B*ecause the Lord is my
Shepherd, I have everything
I need! He lets me rest in the
meadow grass and leads me
beside the quiet streams.
He gives me new strength.

PSALM 23:1-3 TLB

AUGUST 17

*G*od has a thousand ways where
I can see not one;
When all my means have
reached their end
Then His have just begun.

ESTHER GUYOT

MAY 17

Our joy will be complete if we remain in His love—for His love is personal, intimate, real, living, delicate, faithful love.

MOTHER TERESA

AUGUST 16

*G*od will
never, never let us
down if we have faith and put our
trust in Him. He will always
look after us.

MOTHER TERESA

MAY 18

*B*eauty's tears are lovelier
than her smile.

CAMPBELL

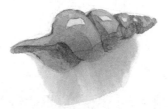

AUGUST 15

*L*isten to me...you whom I have upheld since you were conceived, and have carried since your birth. Even to your old age and gray hairs I am he, I am he who will sustain you. I have made you and I will carry you.

ISAIAH 46:3-4 NIV

MAY 19

One cannot collect all the beautiful shells on the beach. One can collect only a few, and they are more beautiful if they are few.

ANNE MORROW LINDBERGH

AUGUST 14

We can make up our minds
whether our lives in this world
shall...be beautiful and fragrant
like the lilies of the field.

FATHER ANDREW SDC

MAY 20

When God has become our
shepherd, our refuge, our fortress,
then we can reach out to Him
in the midst of a broken world
and feel at home while
still on the way.

HENRI J. M. NOUWEN

AUGUST 13

*C*haracter cannot be developed
in ease and quiet. Only through the
experience of trial and suffering
can the soul be strengthened,
vision cleared, ambition inspired,
and success achieved.

HELEN KELLER

MAY 21

*Y*our love, O Lord, reaches to
the heavens, your faithfulness
to the skies.... How priceless
is your unfailing love!

PSALM 36:5,7 NIV

AUGUST 12

*T*hrough the heartfelt
mercies of our God,
God's Sunrise will
break in upon us,
Shining on those in the darkness...
Then showing us the way,
one foot at a time,
down the path of peace.

LUKE 1:78-79 MSG

MAY 22

Lord, help me realize that I am not the only one hurting...that we all have pain in our lives. May I listen...comfort...and give unconditional love to all who pass my way.

CAROL HAMBLET ADAMS

AUGUST 11

*B*roken shells are shells that
have been tested...and tried...and
hurt...yet they don't quit.
They continue to be.
Thank You, Lord, for the great
strength it takes to simply be.

CAROL HAMBLET ADAMS

MAY 23

There are moments when our hearts nearly burst within us for the sheer joy of being alive. The first sight of our newborn babies, the warmth of love in another's eyes, the fresh scent of rain on a hot summer's eve—moments like these renew in us a heartfelt appreciation for life.

GWEN WEISING

AUGUST 10

*W*e do not understand the intricate pattern of the stars in their courses, but we know that He who created them does, and that just as surely as He guides them, He is charting a safe course for us.

— BILLY GRAHAM

MAY 24

The ordinary acts we practice
every day at home are of more
importance to the soul than their
simplicity might suggest.

THOMAS MOORE

AUGUST 9

Thank You, Lord, for being with me to share my life...to help me carry my burdens.

CAROL HAMBLET ADAMS

MAY 25

*S*omething deep in all of us
yearns for God's beauty, and
we can find it no matter
where we are.

Sue Monk Kidd

AUGUST 8

*H*e who has God and
everything has no more than
he who has God alone.

C. S. LEWIS

MAY 26

No eye has seen, nor ear heard,
nor the human heart conceived,
what God has prepared for
those who love him.

1 CORINTHIANS 2:9 NRSV

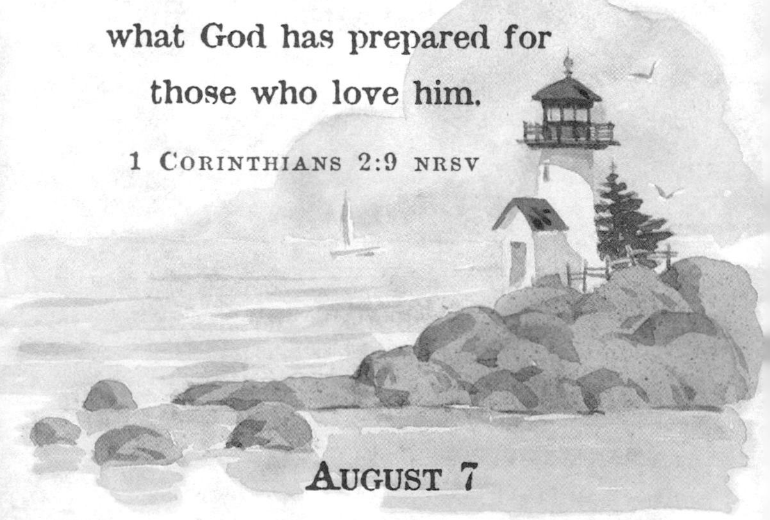

AUGUST 7

*H*ope does not necessarily take
the form of excessive confidence;
rather, it involves the simple
willingness to take the next step.

STANLEY HAUERWAS

MAY 27

The light of
God surrounds me,
The love of God enfolds me,
The presence of God protects me,
God is always with me.

AUGUST 6

*A*nd when the storm is passed, the brightness for which He is preparing us will shine out unclouded, and it will be Himself.

MORROW COFFEY GRAHAM

MAY 28

The brook would lose its song if
we removed the rocks.

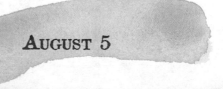

AUGUST 5

My God is changeless in his love for me and he will come and help me.

PSALM 59:10 TLB

MAY 29

*S*tand outside this evening.
Look at the stars. Know that
you are special and
loved by the
One who
created them.

AUGUST 4

How calm,—how beautiful
comes on
The stilly hour, when
storms have gone,
When warring winds
have died away
And clouds, beneath
the dancing ray
Melt off and leave
the land and sea,
Sleeping in bright tranquillity.

MOORE

MAY 30

$\mathcal{L}$et your faith be
in the quiet confidence
that God will every day and
every moment keep you
as the apple of His eye.

ANDREW MURRAY

AUGUST 3

Love is never lost.
If not reciprocated, it will
flow back and soften and
purify the heart.

WASHINGTON IRVING

May 31

I call to God, I cry to God to help me. From his palace he hears my call; my cry brings me right into his presence— a private audience!

PSALM 18:6 MSG

AUGUST 2

The rainbow of God's promises
is always above the trials
and storms
of life.

CHARLES SHEPSON

JUNE 1

*J*oys come from simple and natural things: mists over meadows, sunlight on leaves, the path of the moon over water.

SIGURD F. OLSON

AUGUST 1

*F*aith is the bird that feels the
light when the dawn is still dark.

RABINDRANATH TAGORE

JUNE 2

*W*hen you get into a tight place and everything goes against you, till it seems as though you could not hang on a minute longer, never give up then, for that is just the place and time that the tide will turn.

HARRIET BEECHER STOWE

JULY 31

*S*atisfy us in
our earliest youth
with your
lovingkindness, giving us constant
joy to the end of our lives.

PSALM 90:14 TLB

JUNE 3

There is no better exercise for
the heart than reaching down
and lifting someone up.

JULY 30

As a rose fills a room with
its fragrance, so will God's
love fill our lives.

MARGARET BROWNLEY

JUNE 4

*T*he God who created, names, and numbers the stars in the heavens also numbers the hairs of my head.... He pays attention to very big things and to very small ones. What matters to me matters to Him, and that changes my life.

ELISABETH ELLIOT

JULY 29

*B*e like the bird that,
halting on its flight
Awhile on boughs too slight,
Feels them give way beneath her,
and yet sings
Knowing that she hath wings.

VICTOR HUGO

JUNE 5

$\mathcal{N}$ot one is missing, not one
forgotten. God the Father has
his eye on each of you.... May
everything good from
God be yours!

1 Peter 1:1-2 MSG

July 28

When we call on God, He bends down His ear to listen, as a father bends down to listen to his little child.

ELIZABETH CHARLES

JUNE 6

*I*f you can't pray as you want to,
pray as you can. God knows
what you mean.

VANCE HAVNER

JULY 27

*P*eace I leave with you, my peace I give unto you.... Let not your heart be troubled, neither let it be afraid.

JOHN 14:27 KJV

JUNE 7

Lord, help me to reach out to others...especially to the broken and discouraged...not only to love them, but to learn from them as well.

CAROL HAMBLET ADAMS

JULY 26

*Lord, when I hurt, may I be
strong enough to show my pain
and brokenness like this shell.
May I give myself permission to
hurt...to cry...to be human.*

CAROL HAMBLET ADAMS

JUNE 8

*W*e may depend upon God's
promises, for He will be
as good as His word.

MATTHEW HENRY

JULY 25

*T*he best things are nearest:
breath in your nostrils, light in
your eyes, flowers at your feet,
duties at your hand, the path
of God just before you.

ROBERT LOUIS STEVENSON

JUNE 9

Like the azure ocean swelling,
like the jewel all-excelling,
far beyond our human telling,
is the perfect peace of God.

MICHAEL PERRY

JULY 24

*L*ove, consolation, and peace
bloom only in the garden
of sweet contentment.

MARTHA ANDERSON

JUNE 10

*A*s high as the heavens are
above the earth, so great
is his love.

PSALM 103:11 NIV

JULY 23

$\mathcal{F}$ew things heal wounded spirits
better than the balm of
a supportive embrace.

CHARLES R. SWINDOLL

JUNE 11

You can choose to make a separate peace.... At the very simplest level, you find a place to retreat. You arrange for a refuge where you can rest and be renewed before returning to the fray. Your corner may be as simple as a comfortable chair.

THOMAS KINKADE

JULY 22

*T*here is joy in heaven when
a tear of sorrow is shed in the
presence of a truly understanding
heart. And heaven will
never forget that joy.

CHARLES MALIK

JUNE 12

*W*hen life
becomes all snarled
up, offer it to God and let Him
untie the knots.

JULY 21

Let him have all your worries
and cares, for he is always
thinking about you and watching
everything that concerns you.

1 PETER 5:7 TLB

JUNE 13

*N*othing can separate you from
God's love, absolutely nothing....
God is enough for time,
God is enough for eternity.
God is enough!

HANNAH WHITALL SMITH

JULY 20

*G*od has a purpose for your life,
and no one else can
take your place.

JUNE 14

Our strength often increases
in proportion to the
obstacles
imposed upon it.

PAUL DE RAPIN

JULY 19

*R*est is not idleness, and to lie
sometimes on the grass under the
trees on a summer's day, listening
to the murmur of water, or
watching the clouds float across
the sky, is by no means
a waste of time.

JOHN LUBBOCK

JUNE 15

I have learned to be content whatever the circumstances. I know what it is to be in need, and I know what it is to have plenty. I have learned the secret of being content.

PHILIPPIANS 4:11-12 NIV

JULY 18

Little drops
of water,
little grains of sand,
Make the mighty ocean
and the pleasant land.
Little deeds of kindness,
little words of love,
Help to make earth happy
like the Heaven above.

JULIA FLETCHER CARNEY

JUNE 16

The firmest friendships have
been formed in mutual adversity,
as iron is most strongly welded
by the fiercest fire.

JULY 17

*T*here are vast, untapped resources of faith...and talent...that can only be discovered in adversity!

DR. ROBERT SCHULLER

JUNE 17

*W*hatever happens, do not lose
hold of the two main ropes of
life—hope and faith.

JULY 16

*I*s anyone crying for help? God is listening, ready to rescue you. If your heart is broken, you'll find God right there.

PSALM 34:17-18 MSG

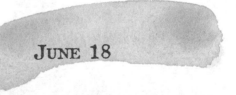

JUNE 18

*O*ne step ahead is all
I now can see,
But He who notes
the sparrow's fall,
He leadeth me.
Not only by the waters still
my feet may tread,
But with my hand in His,
I know that I am led.

Ella B. Doxsee

July 15

$\mathcal{I}$t is the
simple things of
life that make living
worthwhile, the sweet fundamental
things such as love and duty, work
and rest, and living
close to nature.

LAURA INGALLS WILDER

JUNE 19

*G*od walks with us.... He scoops
us up in His arms or simply sits
with us in silent strength until
we cannot avoid the awesome
recognition that yes, even
now, He is here.

GLORIA GAITHER

JULY 14

*The treasure our heart searches
for is found in the ocean of
God's love.*

JANET L. WEAVER

JUNE 20

I will refresh the weary
and satisfy the faint.

JEREMIAH 31:25 NIV

JULY 13

*W*here there is pain, let there be softening. Where there is bitterness, let there be acceptance. Where there is silence, let there be communication. Where there is loneliness, let there be friendships. Where there is despair, let there be hope.

RUTH EISEMAN

JUNE 21

The Lord doesn't always remove
the sources of stress in our
lives...but He's always there and
cares for us. We can feel His arms
around us on the darkest night.

DR. JAMES DOBSON

JULY 12

*O*h, the comfort, the
inexpressible comfort of
feeling safe with a person:
having neither to weigh
thoughts nor measure words,
but to pour them out.

GEORGE ELIOT

JUNE 22

*N*o soul is desolate as long as there is a human being for whom it can feel trust and reverence.

GEORGE ELIOT

JULY 11

You are my refuge and my
shield; I have put my hope
in your word.

PSALM 119:114 NIV

JUNE 23

May I have the courage to risk sharing my feelings with others so that I may receive support and encouragement along the way.

CAROL HAMBLET ADAMS

JULY 10

Thank You, Lord, for filling my life with people who care. Thank You for my family...for my friends...for those who are always there for me.

CAROL HAMBLET ADAMS

JUNE 24

*L*ove means to love that which is unlovable, or it is no virtue at all; forgiving means to pardon that which is unpardonable, or it is no virtue at all—and to hope means hoping when things are hopeless, or it is no virtue at all.

G. K. CHESTERTON

JULY 9

We are all precious
in God's sight.

JUNE 25

He surrounds me with
lovingkindness and tender mercies.
He fills my life with good things!

PSALM 103:4-5 TLB

JULY 8

$\mathcal{F}$aith and doubt both are needed—not as antagonists, but working side by side—to take us around the unknown curve.

LILLIAN SMITH

JUNE 26

*C*hallenges are like summer
storms. Everything is more
beautiful when they
have passed.

JULY 7

*I*n God's wisdom, He frequently
chooses to meet our needs by
showing His love toward us
through the hands and
hearts of others.

JACK HAYFORD

JUNE 27

*P*rayer is kind of like calling home every day.

BARBARA JOHNSON

JULY 6

*T*he Lord your God...will take
great delight in you, he will quiet
you with his love, he will rejoice
over you with singing.

ZEPHANIAH 3:17 NIV

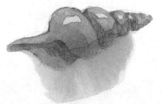

JUNE 28

*M*ay I never
miss a sunset or a
rainbow because I am
looking down.

JULY 5

Everyone was meant to share
God's all-abiding love and care;
He saw that we would
need to know
a way to let these feelings show....
So God made hugs.

JILL WOLF

JUNE 29

*S*ummer afternoon—summer afternoon; to me those have always been the two most beautiful words in the English language.

HENRY JAMES

JULY 4

$\mathcal{S}$ome people make the world
special just by being in it.

JUNE 30

$\mathcal{T}$he Lord longs to be gracious
to you; he rises to show you
compassion....
Blessed are all
who wait
for him!

ISAIAH 30:18 NIV

JULY 3

$\mathcal{J}$know not where
His islands lift
Their fronded palms in air;
I only know I cannot drift
Beyond His love and care.

JOHN GREENLEAF WHITTIER

JULY 1

*H*is tenderness
in the springing grass,
His beauty in the flowers,
His living love in
the sun above—
All here, and near, and ours.

CHARLOTTE PERKINS GILMAN

JULY 2